Nothing's more important to Nick, Sam, Justin, and Dennis than their team, the Alden Panthers. Whether the sport is football, basketball, baseball, or soccer, the four seventh-graders can always be found practicing, sweating, and giving their all. Sometimes the Panthers are on their way to a winning season, and sometimes the team can't do anything right. But no matter what, you can be sure the ALDEN ALL STARS are playing to win.

Chock-full of plays, sports details, and plenty of exciting sports action, the ALDEN ALL STARS series is just right for anyone who loves to compete—or just loves a good story.

ALDEN ALL STARS

Duel on the Diamond

Tommy Hallowell

PUFFIN BOOKS

PUFFIN BOOKS
Published by the Penguin Group
Viking Penguin, a division of Penguin Books USA Inc.,
40 West 23rd Street, New York, New York 10010, U.S.A.
Penguin Books Ltd, 27 Wrights Lane, London W8 5TZ, England
Penguin Books Australia Ltd, Ringwood, Victoria, Australia
Penguin Books Canada Ltd, 2801 John Street, Markham, Ontario, Canada L3R 1B4
Penguin Books (N.Z.) Ltd, 182–190 Wairau Road, Auckland 10, New Zealand

Penguin Books Ltd, Registered Offices: Harmondsworth, Middlesex, England

First published in Puffin Books 1990
1   3   5   7   9   10   8   6   4   2
Copyright © Daniel Weiss and Associates, 1990
All rights reserved

LIBRARY OF CONGRESS CATALOGING IN PUBLICATION DATA
Hallowell, Tommy.   Duel on the diamond.
Summary: Four junior high school friends find their
"war" with another clique of boys is costing their base-
ball team a championship season.
[1. Baseball—Fiction]   I. Title.
PZ7.H164Du   1990   [Fic]   89-10922
ISBN 0-14-032910-2

Printed in the United States of America
Set in Century Schoolbook

*To Pepi Baptiste: shortstop, point guard,
quarterback, and Latin scholar.*

1

Dennis knew the runner wanted to steal.

Crouched behind home plate, Dennis could see him stalking off the first base bag, eyeing the pitcher, digging at the loose infield dirt with his cleats. It was obvious. Duane Potter wanted to run.

Dennis Clements was playing catcher in today's scrimmage game and he would be the catcher when the Alden Junior High seventh-grade team played their first game next Wednesday. Coach Lanigan had announced the starting lineup at the beginning

1

of practice that afternoon. For Dennis, the lineup was all good news; his three best friends were all starters, too. Sam McCaskill at pitcher or shortstop, Nick Wilkerson in centerfield, and Justin Johnson at second base.

Even assured of a starting slot, Dennis wasn't relaxing a bit. He had made it this far on pure hustle. He didn't have all the natural talent in the world, but he made up the difference with extra effort. That was how he had been the football team's star linebacker, even though he was average size. He loved competition and he loved a challenge.

At the moment, he had one. Duane Potter had pretty good speed, a decent set of wheels. All Dennis could think about was throwing him out at second. He even hoped Duane would try to steal. It was near the end of practice and he was tired, but Dennis was determined not to let the runner advance. He could sense that Potter was challenging him. They were playing a little game within the game. It was a matter of pride.

Dennis put his hand down to call the pitch. Sam was on the mound and Kyle Bushmiller was hitting. Kyle stepped into the box, placing his feet carefully in the worn dirt. Dennis put down one finger, the signal for the fastball. Sam gave a small nod, glanced at first, and set. He threw. Out of the corner of his eye, Dennis saw Duane bluff toward second, but stop. The pitch was way outside the strike zone. Dennis backhanded it and Coach Lanigan, who was acting as plate umpire, called it a ball.

Sam missed with a change-up next, then got Kyle to swing and miss at a high fastball. Duane still hadn't taken off, but Dennis figured he wouldn't wait much longer. He thought of calling a pitchout, but Sam was having too much trouble throwing strikes. So Dennis called for the fastball. He would have the ball quickly, and the sooner he got it, the sooner he could throw down to second.

Sam went into his windup. Dennis got way down, setting a low target with his glove. If Kyle swung, Dennis hoped to make him swing down and hit a grounder, maybe hit into a double play. As Sam released the ball, Duane took off. The ball came in too low, so Kyle didn't swing. Dennis snatched the pitch and came up firing.

The moment Dennis made the throw, he knew it was a good one. He had found the ball in his glove quickly, turned it to find a seam with his finger—to get good control—and snapped it away.

The throw was right on the mark, just a bit toward the first base side of second. Barry caught the ball and dropped the tag well in front of Duane's slide. Coach Lanigan called him out.

Dennis felt the thrill of success. He punched the air with his hand, and celebrated with a little stutter step. Then he noticed that Duane was watching him. In fact, Duane was doing more than watching, he was really giving him the evil eye. *Geez,* thought Dennis, *what's the big deal?* He looked over at Duane again, who was still staring at him. Dennis didn't know quite what to make of it. This was just practice, after all. If Duane couldn't take a little ribbing, well, tough luck. Anyway, Dennis had other things to worry about, like how Sam ought to pitch Kyle now that the count was three balls and a strike.

They had no choice but to come across with a strike. Dennis set a target in the middle of the plate. Sam threw it right down Broadway, and, naturally enough, Kyle smacked it deep to the alley between left and center.

Practice games are funny, thought Dennis as he watched Kyle speed around first while Nick and Mitch both scampered after the ball. You do your best to get the guys out, but when they do get hits, well, that was a good thing, too. Kyle ended up at third. It was no surprise. Kyle was by far the team's best hitter, both for power and average. All through Little League he had been the best. Dennis was just glad they were going to be on the same team this year.

After another inning, Coach called it a day. Sam looked relieved as he came in from the mound.

"What's the matter, Ace? Tired?" Dennis kidded him.

"Oh, man," was all Sam could manage. Nick jogged up to join them as they walked off the field.

"What are you complaining about?" Dennis said. "Try squatting two hundred times. I'm the guy who should be moaning."

"Yeah, but you volunteered to play catcher," Nick said, "and that makes you certifiably nuts."

"Crazy, you bet. Let's go run some wind sprints," Dennis said, running a quick circle around his friends. They just laughed.

"Hey, I almost forgot it's Friday," Sam said. "Tonight Mr. Wilkerson is taking us out for burgers."

Nick's father had offered to take his son's friends out for a fast food dinner on the way home from practice. The thought made them walk faster. Nick, Dennis, Justin, and Sam went way back together. They had met up in the fourth grade at Fairwood

Elementary and had been tight ever since. When they arrived at Alden that fall they were psyched: organized sports at last! They had all played on the football team, with Sam battling to become the starting quarterback. The Alden basketball team, with Dennis and Nick leading them, had had a tough battle for the league title. Justin hadn't made the final basketball cuts, but he had stuck with the team as manager. It was still chilly out, but spring was in the air, and baseball was on.

Mr. Wilkerson was standing by the fence that surrounded the field. As the others went to join him, Dennis had to detour to the dugout to pack up his equipment—shin guards, chest protector, mask, gloves. As he ducked into the dugout, he heard Nick yell: "Dennis said we should go on without him."

"You do and I'll rearrange your faces!" Dennis yelled back, as he packed up. Even though all this extra equipment was sometimes a drag, Dennis was glad that he had "volunteered" to play catcher. He had sometimes played behind the plate back in Little League, and once he had gotten over being afraid of foul tips, he had liked it. Wearing all the equipment was cool, and one thing about playing catcher, it was never boring. There was no time to daydream behind the plate.

After a few minutes Justin joined his friends and they piled into the station wagon and drove into downtown Cranbrook to McDonald's. They were hungry. Practicing in the chilly weather of early spring really worked up their appetites, so when they got to their table the conversation stopped until the first burgers were nearly gone.

"Whoa," Mr. Wilkerson said, stirring his coffee. "What is this? A feeding frenzy?"

All they could do was grin, because all four of their mouths were full. They made an effort to slow down but picked at the last french fries and slurped the ends of their shakes before they started gabbing. Dennis set down his drink first.

"This baseball season is going to be the best."

"Yeah, all four of us on the starting team," Sam said.

"We were all on the football team," Justin noted.

"Except we played some on offense, some on defense," Dennis said. "It wasn't like this. And there were so many guys on the football team, you know?"

"I still can't believe that Coach Lanigan made me a starter," Justin said. "Mitch is better."

"No way," said Sam. "You worked hard, you deserved it."

The others agreed. Only Dennis thought Justin

might be right. It was great that they were all starters, but Justin had a point about Mitch Tompkins. Mitch was a really smooth fielder, and it was a close call on who was the better hitter. Dennis figured Coach must know what he was doing, but he wondered if Coach was playing favorites.

"Maybe I'm just a nicer guy than Mitch," Justin said with a laugh.

"That wouldn't be too hard," Nick said. "You ever seen that guy smile? I haven't."

"Yeah, not too friendly," Sam agreed.

"All right," Nick said. "Let's get down to it. Who's the biggest jerk on the team? Let's vote."

"The biggest jerk? It's gotta be *you*, Nick," Dennis laughed.

"Not including me," Nick said.

"Maybe Brad McCarthy?" Sam suggested.

"No way," Dennis said shaking his head. "He's just really shy. What about Barry Sanderson, or Duane."

"Barry can be a pain," Justin said, "but at least he's pretty funny sometimes."

"Why does anyone on the team have to be a jerk?" asked Mr. Wilkerson.

"They don't have to be, Dad," Nick said. "They just are."

Everyone laughed. They all agreed that even if the other guys on the team weren't their favorite people, the four of them playing baseball together was the greatest. They only had to do one more thing to make it perfect—win the league championship.

2

Barry threw the pitch. The Bradley batter watched it go by, waist-high, and Dennis caught it. "Strike!" Dennis held the ball for a moment in one hand, giving it a shake in Barry's direction to signify that it was a good pitch.

It wasn't much of a day for baseball, but at least it wasn't raining. The afternoon was cold and gray, still damp from the weekend's rain, and, for the Alden Panthers baseball squad, it was opening day.

The next pitch came in higher, but this time the kid took a cut and missed. Strike two.

Bradley Junior High had traveled to Cranbrook for the game. The Alden players had been glad to see Bradley arrive at four o'clock. They could stop trying to get the infield into decent shape, sweeping away puddles, spreading dry dirt and pounding it flat. They were glad to hang up their rakes and get out their gloves.

Barry's third pitch was even higher, but the batter went for it again. Not a chance. Strike three and the first out of the season. Dennis jumped up and threw the ball around the horn.

Barry Sanderson was the starting pitcher. The league rules limited pitchers to seven innings a week. It was supposed to keep kids from hurting their arms. Since the team usually played two seven-inning games each week, that meant they needed two starting pitchers. Coach Lanigan had chosen Barry and Sam. They would alternate. If either one got into trouble, Duane, Justin, and Kyle were all available for relief pitching.

Barry walked the second batter, but the third man popped up and the fourth hit a grounder to Justin, who made the easy play to first. Now it was time for Alden to take their first licks.

Nick was the lead-off batter. The Bradley pitcher started out wild, walking Nick on four straight pitches. The Alden bench started hooting.

"Somebody show him home plate!"

"No pitcher! No pitcher!"

Duane took a called third strike, and Barry hit into a force at second but beat out the double play attempt. So with two outs and a man on, Kyle came up. Sure enough, he showed why they call the fourth slot "cleanup." Kyle knocked a double to the fence and Barry scored easily. But that was all the scoring. Sam, up next, hit a pop fly to center.

Alden's 1–0 lead disappeared fast. With two outs, the big Bradley first baseman took a fastball over the fence for a home run. Barry was peeved. Dennis jogged out to the mound to help him cool down.

"Hey, don't worry about it. You made a good pitch," Dennis said.

"Yeah, right," Barry answered abruptly, putting out his glove for the ball without even looking up.

Dennis went back to his position. He was thinking that he still had a lot to learn about handling pitchers. What should he say to a guy like Barry, who got so angry at himself for one mistake?

Larry Stiles bobbled a ball at third for an error.

Barry gave up a single, but he managed to get out of the inning without surrendering another run.

After Larry hit a liner right at the Bradley shortstop for the first out, Dennis stepped up to the plate for his first at bat of the season. He looked out at the pitcher. He noticed for the first time that the opposing pitcher was chewing gum. Dennis shifted his weight, gave the bat a little half-swing, and then readied himself.

The pitch came and Dennis swung, missing the low ball by at least six inches. It was way out of the strike zone. *Dumb, dumb, dumb!* he thought. *Don't be over-anxious!*

The next pitch came right across for a called strike. He was down in the count, 0–2. Now he had to protect the plate. On the next pitch he connected, barely.

As the ball left the bat he figured it was an infield fly, but as he watched, running hard to first, he saw that it was beyond the infield! It was a dying quail that was going to drop in. Then he saw something else: the shortstop and second baseman were both chasing the ball and no one was covering second!

The ball dropped and Dennis never stopped running. The center fielder picked up the ball and threw it in to the pitcher, who had finally run to cover second. But it was too late as Dennis slid in safely. A blooper turned into a hustling double! Dennis loved it. After advancing to third on Alan Broadstreet's fly out, Dennis was stranded when Justin grounded out.

In the top of the fourth, with two men on, the Bradley first baseman hit a long double to score two runs. Bradley took a 3–1 lead. Alden pushed one across in the fifth, but in the top of the seventh— and final—inning Bradley still had a one-run lead.

The first Bradley batter tried to bunt for a base hit, but Dennis jumped on the ball quickly and threw him out easily. Then Barry walked a man and the next batter pulled a change-up for a single. A pop fly in the infield made it two outs with runners on the corners. But trouble was up next: the big Bradley first baseman.

The first pitch was an outside fastball that he hit for a long foul. The next two were balls, not even close. Dennis got into his crouch and called for another fastball. Barry shook off the sign. Dennis put down two fingers, for the change-of-pace pitch. Barry again shook him off. He could put down a closed fist, but that was the signal to throw to first and if Barry wanted to do that he would do it on his own. Dennis stood up. What was Barry doing? He only *had* two pitches. He threw two kinds of fastballs, one with the seams and one across the seams, and he threw the slower pitch to keep batters off balance, but that was it. Dennis jogged out to the mound.

"What's up?"

"I'm gonna throw a curve."

"What?"

"Three fingers, curve. Got it?"

"Coach Lanigan said no breaking balls—it's bad for your arm."

"What are you gonna do, Mr. All-American, tell on me?"

"No, I . . ."

"Three fingers, curve."

Dennis gave up. He didn't really care if Barry threw a curve, but why be such a jerk about it.

Behind the plate, Dennis put down three fingers and Barry nodded. The pitch was a good one and it actually did seem to break down a little. Anyway, it was good enough because the batter swung and missed, bringing the count to 2–2.

Dennis called for the fastball, then the change. Barry shook him off both times. He wanted to throw another curve. Dennis gave him the sign and got into ready position. The pitch came, this one slower than the last, and waist high. The kid powdered it.

15

Nick, out in center, didn't even run. Like everyone, he just turned and watched it go. Dennis had never seen anyone his age hit a ball that far. Bradley led 6–2.

The next batter grounded out and the inning was over. Dennis found himself jogging past Barry and, still peeved about his attitude, couldn't resist making a crack.

"Nice curveball."

Barry didn't say a thing.

Three batters and three outs later, the 6–2 score was final and Alden was 0–1.

3

Dennis was used to people liking him. He couldn't think of anyone who had ever had a problem or a fight with him. So it was a shock when Duane Potter punched him in the nose.

Dennis was waiting in the hot lunch line outside the lunchroom, wishing he were closer in line to Samantha Meyers, when a couple of eighth-grade guys he didn't know rushed by. At that moment Duane came around the corner. It was a collision course. The bigger guys kept running, dashing around Duane, but in the process they knocked his notebook out of his hands. Papers went flying everywhere. Looking back, the guys just laughed and kept going. Duane was okay, just surprised and embarrassed to have had this happen in front of the whole line of people.

Dennis couldn't help laughing—a little too loudly. That was all it took.

Duane left his papers scattered where they had fallen, walked right over and said: "Think that's funny?"

"I'm sorry, Duane, it's just . . ." Dennis began, but by then the balled fist was on its way. Dennis just had time to roll his head with the punch, but it still hurt. Duane caught him full on the nose and then the back of Dennis's head hit the wall.

Dennis hadn't been in a real fight before, but he had watched enough cop shows to have a pretty good idea what to do. In a flash he was on Duane and the two flailed at each other in a quick series of wild punches, while the crowd of students around them yelled and cheered. Finally, a cafeteria monitor and a cafeteria worker dragged them apart.

Breathing heavily, Dennis looked at Duane.

"What's your problem!"

"You're my problem, you little . . ."

"You're a moron."

Dennis sized up the damage. His nose was throbbing, and putting his wrist to his nose, he discovered it was also bleeding. The knuckles on his right hand hurt from a punch he had launched into Duane's mouth. Other than a few scratches, that was all. He felt a little stupid being held by the back of his shirt now. He wondered what would happen next. Probably a visit to Mr. Dreben, the vice principal who always seemed to be in charge of handing out punishments. Seeing him seemed a lot worse than a bloody nose.

Sure enough, they were marched to Mr. Dreben's office. He was talking to someone, so Duane and Dennis were left sitting in a waiting area under the supervision of the secretary. Dennis's nose had stopped bleeding. Duane was holding some ice in a cloth to his cut lip. Dennis was still baffled by the whole situation.

"Why did you come after me, Duane?"

"Why? I don't like your haircut. I don't like your preppy shirt and I don't like you and your little jock gang."

Dennis didn't have to glance down to know that

he was wearing an alligator shirt, and he wore his hair short because he liked it that way.

"And that's reason to punch a guy?"

"Reason enough."

Dennis just shook his head. He didn't want to be best friends with Duane, but he wished they hadn't fought. They were teammates after all. But what could he do?

Mr. Dreben and a teacher came out of his office. The teacher left and the secretary explained who Dennis and Duane were in a low voice. Without saying a word, Mr. Dreben led them into his office, had them sit down, and sat down himself, behind a large desk. He sat there silent for what seemed like forever. Dennis fidgeted in his seat and he saw that Duane looked uneasy, too. Finally, Mr. Dreben spoke.

"Duane Potter and Dennis Clements. As you both know, this is unacceptable behavior. Especially you, Mr. Potter. It seems to me that you've already had the opportunity to hear my little lecture on fighting. Yes?"

"Yes, sir."

"Would you like to tell me why this fight occurred? I'll give you each a chance. Duane?"

They each explained, Duane saying that Dennis

was laughing at him, Dennis saying he was attacked for no reason. But Mr. Dreben didn't really seem to care whose fault it was. After they were done, he gave them a serious talk about maturity and handling disagreements. Then he got down to the punishment.

"I understand that both of you are playing baseball this spring."

They nodded. He knew more about them than Dennis would have guessed.

"And you know that being on the baseball team is a privilege, a privilege that can be taken away."

They nodded again, a little more slowly. Their eyes widened a bit, too. *He wouldn't,* thought Dennis.

"I don't intend to do that."

A look of relief came over the faces of both Dennis and Duane.

"But if necessary, I will. Be assured of that."

The boys nodded.

"In the meantime, you'll be joining me for detention for the next week. I'm really disappointed that two teammates couldn't settle their differences in a more civilized way."

At that Mr. Dreben again let them sit silently for a long pause. Dennis was starting to wonder if he was going to have time to get any lunch before the

period was over, but Mr. Dreben finally made the
boys shake hands and then let them go with just
enough time left to grab some lunch.

The only problem was trying to eat while his
friends were asking him all about the fight. Nick,
Sam, Justin, Kyle, and Jimmy Carlisle were gathered around him, trying to get what details they
could. Only Justin had actually seen any of the short
encounter, and he had only seen the tail end.

Dennis tried not to make a big deal about it, but
he also wanted to make sure that everyone knew
that he had done okay in the actual fight.

"He was holding me by the shirt, but I got my
hand free and caught him in the mouth," he said,
showing his cut knuckle. "Then I put a leg sweep on
him and knocked him down, but that was when they
grabbed us."

"But why did he come at you?" Sam asked.

"Ask *him* that. . . . I couldn't help laughing
when his papers went flying. A lot of people were
laughing."

"He's a thug," Justin said.

"Think you hurt him?" Sam asked.

"No brain, no pain," Nick quipped before Dennis
could answer. They all laughed.

The guys basically agreed that it was Duane's

fault, but of course, they were Dennis's friends. At another table on the other side of the cafeteria, they could see Duane with his friends—Barry, Mitch, Brad McCarthy, Paul Dominick and some others—and they all knew he was telling his side of the story.

4

Alden was a lot like every junior high. It had seventh and eighth grades, librarians with thick glasses, not enough dances, a tough vice principal, hall lockers that could be popped open if you hit them just right, jocks, nerds, brains, and every sort of "popular" group.

Sam, Dennis, Nick, and Justin had stuck together all through their years at Fairwood Elementary and now they were sticking together at Alden. Even though they weren't in all the same classes anymore, they found plenty of opportunities to hang out. After school, in the lunchroom, during practice— they were always loud, sometimes funny, never apart.

"I would say that we're 'popular,' " Sam said. The four friends were sitting in the cafeteria killing time before homeroom.

"Yeah, but what does that mean?" Justin asked. "None of us has a girlfriend."

"But we could," Sam said. "We could easily get girls to go to a dance with us."

"So that makes us popular?" Dennis asked.

"Yeah, I don't get it," Nick said. "Does 'popular' mean that four out of five kids surveyed would choose us over another group?"

They laughed.

"Sort of," Sam said. "It's like, well just think of examples. I'll tell you if they're popular or not."

"Guys?" Dennis asked.

"Yeah."

"Milo Svenson," Nick said and the others all laughed again. Milo was the exact opposite of pop- ular. He was the geekiest of the nerds. The nerd king.

"Kyle Bushmiller," Justin suggested.

"Hmm, that's tough," Sam said. "He's such a good athlete he could be, but he's such a loner, you know? Shy. I'd say no."

"Dave Zinsser," Dennis said.

"Yeah, Dave's all right, yes."

"How about Duane?"

"Potter, no. You've gotta be athletic *and* do okay in school. He's in remedial math and stuff, I think."

"But he's got a girlfriend," Justin said.

"Who?" Sam asked.

"Marilyn Stevens."

"No, really?"

"Yeah, it's true. She's not bad."

"Still, he's not in a popular group, so he's not popular," Sam insisted.

"So Barry and Paul and all those guys . . ."

"Unpopular."

"Sounds like you have to be friends with Sam McCaskill to be popular," Dennis said.

"Yeah, that's the basic rule," Sam agreed, laughing at himself.

"Now let me get this straight," Nick said. "You have to be cool to be popular. But you can be cool, but not popular, like Kyle. But tell me this, can you be popular, but not cool?"

26

"Naturally," Sam said. "What do you think you are?"

"Burn!" Justin laughed.

The bell for homeroom rang, so the conversation came to an end.

Dennis had to attend the second day of his detention that afternoon, which meant sitting in the library and studying silently while Mr. Dreben watched. So instead of getting to practice early and throwing the ball around, he arrived when things were already in full swing. Guys were loosening up. Some were playing pepper: one guy hitting soft grounders and liners while the others fielded and quickly tossed the ball back for him to hit again.

Dennis found Sam, Nick, and Justin sitting in the stands talking with Coach Lanigan. He joined them. Coach was really easy to talk to and he had a million baseball stories.

"How was detention?" Nick asked.

"A million laughs."

"We told Coach about the fight," Sam said.

"Fight? It was no fight, it was an attack."

"Don't worry about it, Dennis," Coach said with a smile. "I've got a pretty good idea what happened. But we're going to let bygones be bygones, aren't we?"

Dennis nodded.

"So Justin, you ready to pitch tomorrow?" Coach asked.

"But Sam's starting. . . ."

"Yeah, I mean *after* he gets knocked around in the first inning."

"Even my own coach has no faith," Sam said.

"So is North Colby good?" Justin asked.

"Joe Robinson runs a good program over there, sure."

"Who's the best team?" Dennis asked.

"Well, the guy who coaches Williamsport claims he's got a real phenom for a pitcher, some kid named Dizzy or something," Coach replied, then he stood up. "Why don't you guys quit sitting around gabbing and go warm up. Can't you see I'm busy?"

They all laughed and climbed down from the bleachers. Dennis strapped on his shin guards and grabbed his glove. He saw that Larry Stiles had a ball and seemed to be looking for a throwing partner.

"Hey, Larry, wanna toss?" Dennis asked as he walked to a good throwing distance from him. Larry looked up and took the ball out of his glove, but then changed his mind when he saw it was Dennis.

"Uh, no, here, you can have the ball," Larry said,

giving it a light toss to Dennis. Larry took off his glove and started doing stretching exercises.

Dennis was surprised. He wondered if it had to do with the fight. He didn't think Duane would still be mad at him. So they had a fight, big deal. Nobody hated anybody. Tim Lopatt showed up and he and Dennis threw for a few minutes until Coach Lanigan called everyone in.

"I'm going to work with batters today," Coach said. "Everybody gets two sets of fifteen swings. After that we'll run some infield drills." He called off names to take the field first, and then had everyone spread out to run warm-ups: jumping jacks, hurdler's stretches, the usual stuff.

After that practice was practice. Dennis tried to be particularly chipper, talking it up.

"All right, Justin, bring it across now. Get off your duff, Sam!"

He was still catching when Duane stepped in to take his first round of batting practice. Early, Duane golfed a low pitch, getting a hard liner past first.

"Good hit," Dennis said, but Duane didn't look back or say anything. Dennis thought maybe Duane hadn't heard him.

"Keep your weight back longer, Duane," Coach said. "You're jumping at it."

A few balls later Duane cracked another one, this one deep to left.

"That's it, that's the stuff," Coach encouraged.

"Nice piece of hitting," Dennis said, louder than before.

"I know," Duane said, without looking back. All right, Dennis decided, let him be that way. He didn't care what Duane or anybody else said or did, he wasn't going to get mad.

"All right, last one Duane, lay down a bunt to third," Coach instructed. Duane squared and bunted well. The ball died in the tall grass.

"Beauty," Dennis said.

Duane started to walk behind the cage, past Dennis.

"Thanks, Charlie," Duane said, directly at Dennis.

What the heck is that supposed to mean? Dennis thought. *Charlie?* He didn't know what Duane meant, but he could tell from the wise guy grin on Duane's face that it wasn't meant as a compliment.

5

Saturday, Alden played their second game of the season, at home against North Colby. It was cold, long-underwear weather.

Dennis was glad that Sam was the starting pitcher, because it made his job easy: Sam threw nothing but fastballs, *good* fastballs. He moved the ball around the plate and his throwing motion put a natural movement on the ball. Dennis could forget about calling pitches and think about other things.

Despite the chilly weather, Sam was hot. He retired the first ten batters in order until giving up a flare single in the top of the fourth inning. The runner stole second, despite a decent throw from Dennis, and then scored on a two out single. Sam got out of the inning without any more damage.

Alden had scored twice in the second inning on Nick's single, Duane's walk, and Barry's single that was mishandled by North's right fielder, allowing both runners to come around. So at the end of the fourth the score stood 2–1, Alden.

In the fifth, Sam got into trouble. He was tiring. Two singles and a rare walk loaded the bases with no outs. Coach Lanigan made the slow walk to the mound and took the ball. He called for Duane to shift to pitcher, and Paul Dominick came in to take over first.

Duane was the hardest thrower on the team, but sometimes had trouble with his control. Dennis never looked forward to catching him. It meant leaping at wild pitches and having his hand stung by strikes. Of course, he had to admit that the only thing tougher than catching Duane was hitting against him. If Duane ever got consistent control, no one could deny him a starting slot.

Today he did the job, striking out the first batter and then getting the next man to hit into a tailor-made double play. Alden again failed to score in their half-inning, but at least they went into the last inning still holding a one-run lead. Unfortunately, after getting the first out, Duane walked a batter, who then stole second. This time Dennis made an even better throw and they had him, but the runner's sliding foot knocked the ball out of Alan's glove. Dennis was beginning to think that throwing out runners was impossible. Duane got the next man to pop-up, but then gave up an RBI-single to even the score.

The league rules allowed two extra innings in the event of a tie, but after that, a tie was a tie. Of course, Alden still had the bottom of the sixth to avoid that situation. But a new pitcher came on for North Colby who struck out the side. Nobody was sitting in either dugout as they went into the seventh.

Crouched behind home, Dennis could hear the chatter from both sides.

"No hitter, no hitter!"

"Git 'em, Duane!"

"Give 'em the heat!"

Duane gave up a leadoff double, and the next batter made a good sacrifice bunt to move him to third, but then Duane got a strikeout, a weak grounder, and a pop fly to get out of the jam.

"Yesss! Clutch job!" Barry said, slapping Duane's back as they ran in.

The new North pitcher was invincible. He took the bats out of their hands. Kyle managed to poke a grounder between first and second for a single, but that was all the hitting they could manage. Dennis hit a long fly for the third out.

The top of the eighth was North's last chance to score. Duane got a groundout, but then walked two straight batters. Coach Lanigan came on again, this time calling on Justin. Mitch Tompkins came in to play second.

Justin was the opposite type of pitcher from Duane. He didn't have great velocity. Dennis called Justin's mix of pitches "slow, slower, and slowest." When he got guys out, they usually walked back to the bench wondering how the heck they could have missed those lollipop pitches. The answer was pitch selection and control. Justin was a smart pitcher. He could tell what a hitter's weak spot was—low and inside, away, whatever—and he could put the ball there. The pitch might look as big as a watermelon, but you'd swing and miss it anyway.

Justin took his warm-ups. The runners stood watching on first and second. There was one man out. After his throws, the umpire waved the North

Colby batter into the box and the runners took their leads.

The first pitch was inside for a ball, the next was fouled off to even the count. Dennis could tell that Justin figured this guy was a sucker for a low ball. He crouched way down. The pitch came right to his glove, low, below the strike zone, and sure enough the guy took a cut. He topped the ball, rolling it slowly between the mound and third. Barry, playing third, rushed in, and Justin ran to it, too, but the ball was hit so softly neither of them had a chance. It was a lucky swinging bunt. The bases were loaded—ducks on the pond—with just one out.

The Alden bench grew quiet. Dennis jogged out to the mound.

"He got lucky. You had him nailed," Dennis said. "Just go after this guy."

Justin nodded and took the ball. He looked nervous.

"You got him," Dennis said as he turned toward the plate to go. Then, loudly, to the whole infield, "Let's get two! Turn two."

Justin threw a ball, then another. Behind in the count, he came across with a strike. The hitter got all of it, hammering a screaming line drive that nearly took off Justin's head. All Justin had time to do was duck out of harm's way. It was a hit for sure.

But it wasn't. Mitch, ranging toward the middle, dove for the ball, and not only did he catch it in the air, but he got up and scrambled to second before the runner could get back. It was an unassisted double play, and a game-saver. Dennis and Justin ran out to him excitedly.

"Nice pick!" Justin said gleefully.

"Guess I saved your butt," Mitch responded flatly.

"Guess so," Justin mumbled, his excitement quickly fading. By now, everyone had surrounded Mitch and was drowning him in congratulations as they jogged off the field. Dennis had heard the exchange between Justin and Mitch. In the dugout, he tried to buck up his pitcher, but Justin looked glum, and had no time for encouragement. He was on deck as Brad McCarthy went to bat for Alden's last ups. The worst they could do now was tie—but no one wanted a tie.

Brad went down fighting. He worked to a full count, and fouled off half-a-dozen pitches before he finally lost the battle, grounding out to the first baseman.

Justin shifted his batting helmet on his head, looking uncomfortable as he walked to the plate. The first pitch was across for a called strike. The second was bounced in the dirt, but somehow he had already started to swing and couldn't hold up. Watching from the dugout, Dennis's hopes sank. He could tell that Justin wasn't in control.

"Wait for your pitch!" he yelled.

Justin took an uncertain swing at the very next pitch and whiffed for strike three. The Alden Panthers were down to their last out.

It was the top of the order. Nick stepped to the plate with his usual swagger. The pressure didn't faze him at all. Dennis had to laugh watching him. Nick had a jumpy style at the plate, and a basically good swing, but full of little extra movements: a twitching elbow, a wiggling in his front foot. Coach Lanigan—like every Little League coach Nick had ever had—wanted him to cut it out, but Nick kept falling back into the same habits. In the meantime, he got good results. It was no mistake that Lanigan had given him the number one slot in the batting order.

The first two pitches missed. Nick had a good eye and patience at the plate. He fouled off the third pitch for a strike and then took the third ball. The North pitcher didn't want to walk him, so he threw a sweet potato and Nick crunched it. It was a wicked line drive right at the third baseman, who stuck up his glove in self-defense, and caught it. He looked as surprised as anyone. The game was over.

Nobody was happy with the tie, but nobody was *un*happier than Justin. Normally steady, even quiet, he was really shaken up. He didn't yell, but he moved around quickly, slapping his glove. Dennis caught up with him on their way to the locker room.

"Geez, Justin," he said. "I've never seen you so angry."

"I guess you've never seen me blow a ballgame before either."

"Blow a ballgame? What are you talking about? You pitched great. You kept us in it."

"But I couldn't get a hit in the last inning— couldn't even take a decent swing."

"But you . . ."

"I don't want to talk about it, okay?"

Dennis left him alone.

6

It was nearly the middle of May and the weather was finally beginning to warm up. The edge was off the cold, even first thing in the morning. On Wednesday afternoon Alden played their third game, losing to Lincoln 11–4. It was never close. Barry started and both Duane and Justin worked in relief, but none of them could cool off the bats of their crosstown rival. Kyle went four for four with a homer and Sam hit two doubles, but that was about it for the offense.

On Thursday, taking advantage of the warm

weather, Dennis, Sam, Nick, and Justin rode their bikes to school. Then, after practice, they rode up to the Cranbrook Mall. The plan was to eat dinner and play video games.

Over sandwiches they talked about what they always talked about lately: the team.

"I've officially given up," Justin said. "That talcum powder fight could have been funny, but those guys take everything too far."

"Did you hear that, Dennis?" Sam said. "Justin is giving up. That means you're the last guy who likes Barry's gang."

"I didn't say I liked them, I just don't think we should be feuding with our own team."

"We didn't start it," Nick declared.

"That doesn't mean we can't stop it," Dennis argued.

"But look: they've stopped talking to us, unless it's to make some wisecrack, they sit apart from us, they won't even toss a ball around except with their precious little friends," Sam said. "Plus they're always making jokes about our being Coach's pets and stuff. Who needs it?"

"Yeah, we've given them so many chances," Justin agreed. "I mean, I used to agree with you, Dennis, that we just couldn't take any guff, and maybe we could all play as a team, but it's not going to work. For some reason, they just don't like us. . . ."

"Because we're more popular, smarter, and better looking," Nick interjected.

"Maybe Barry is still mad at me for beating him out at quarterback last fall," Sam said.

"Anyway, they just aren't even going to try to be decent," Justin continued. "Fine. Let them be that way. We just have to play it the same way."

"Look," Dennis said. "I know what jerks they've been. Who got popped by Duane, after all? My nose is still sore. But idiots or not, they're our teammates. We're stuck with them. We don't have to buy them birthday presents, but I still say we've got to get along."

The other three thought it over. Finally, Sam spoke.

"So, how do we get Kyle Bushmiller to be on our side?"

"Yeah," said Nick, "and maybe Bob Donovan."

Dennis rolled his eyes.

"C'mon, Dennis, we don't want to be outnumbered," Nick said. Then he counted on his fingers. "They've got, let's see, Barry, Duane, Paul, Mitch, Alan . . ."

"Larry Stiles," Justin added.

"Larry, right, and Brad. That's seven."

"And besides the four of us," Sam said, "we've got Dave Zinsser and Pete, and maybe Jimmy."

"I don't know about Jimmy," Nick said. "And anyway, those guys aren't as important as Kyle. Kyle's the best player on the team."

"Yeah, but I don't know if Kyle would ever take sides—I don't think he likes anybody."

"Look, Dennis," Justin said. "Baseball isn't a team game like football or basketball. It's really an individual's game, right?"

"What about turning the double play?" Dennis said. "Or throwing out runners? Or the way a pitcher and catcher work together?"

"All right," Justin agreed. "There are a few defensive plays, but really the game boils down to one hitter against one pitcher, one at a time. You know? You take turns. That's ninety percent of the game."

"So what's the point?"

"Point is who cares whether you like Duane or Barry or anybody? You can hate their guts and it won't change a thing on the field," Justin said.

"Well," Dennis admitted grudgingly. "I see your point, but I still think we'd have more fun if we weren't constantly worried about snubbing those guys."

"You know," Sam began. "There is one problem. What about next year?"

"What do you mean?" Justin asked.

"Well, these are a lot of the same guys who were on the basketball team with us, and the football team, and will be again next year."

Justin turned it over in his mind.

"Yeah, that's true," he said, after a moment. "Which is a good reason not to get them really mad. I guess we just have to hope that this is just something about the baseball team."

"Yeah," Nick said, "maybe it won't carry over."

They hadn't thought of this problem before, and it made the whole thing less clear cut. Still, the other three went right back to figuring out how to get Kyle on their side, and guessing which way some of the other "in-betweens"—Jimmy, Tim Lopatt, Jack Sylvester—would go. Dennis went along with the talk, but he still wasn't sure. He sure didn't *like* Duane or Barry, but he hated all the rivalry and fighting that was going on.

They finished eating and headed for the arcade. Dennis soon found himself parked in front of his old favorite, Megatron, blasting photon bandits into the eighth dimension. It helped him relax. When they were all out of quarters they bicycled home. After leaving the others, Dennis thought things over.

Winning the basketball championship had been so great, such a thrill. The Panthers squad had battled as a squad, winning key games down the stretch. Dennis had loved it. Now baseball was a complete letdown. They still hadn't won a game: 0–2–1. Were they that bad? Dennis couldn't help thinking that the losing and the infighting were related.

The problem was that there was nothing he could really do about it. Duane's friends thought that Dennis and his friends were goody-goodies, Coach's pets. It was true that they didn't get into trouble at school or fight much, and it was also true that Coach Lanigan probably did favor them—Dennis remembered the choice of Justin over Mitch at second—but that wasn't their fault. Anyway, there was no way that Dennis could try to be a peacemaker. That was exactly the kind of stuff the other group hated. Dennis couldn't figure his way around it. It was a no-win situation.

In more ways than one.

7

Dennis never wanted to hit someone so much in his life.

Duane just stood there, chewing a huge wad of bubble gum, half-grinning. Every bone in Dennis's body said "hit him" but somehow he didn't. He was too mad even to yell. He just looked into Duane's face and called him the worst thing he could think of. Duane just smiled and chewed, chewed and smiled.

Dennis tried to catch his breath. The ball had hit

him square on the chest. It didn't just sting; it really hurt. Dennis walked off first holding his chest. He knew Duane had done it on purpose.

It was an intrasquad scrimmage game. After knocking a single, Dennis had been at first, where Duane was playing. With two outs, Dennis was looking to steal and Barry, who was pitching, kept close tabs on him. Twice, he threw to first, but each time Dennis got back in time.

The third time he threw, Dennis got back easily. He had hardly been off the bag. Barry had pegged the ball over. This time, instead of catching it, Duane had *purposely*—Dennis was sure—dipped his glove and missed the ball. The throw went right by his glove and before Dennis even had time to think it plunked hard off his chest.

Coach Lanigan had not been watching, but now he saw that Dennis was hurt and jogged over.

"What happened?"

"Got hit, hit by the throw," Dennis said, still wincing.

"Where?"

Dennis showed him.

"Okay, catch your breath, Dennis. It'll be sore, but it'll be all right."

Then Lanigan checked his watch.

"All right, it's five-thirty. Let's bring it in."

The Friday afternoon scrimmage game had started out as a treat, a chance to relax and have some fun instead of running more drills. But Coach Lanigan had let Sam and Barry choose, so the two teams were almost exactly the two rival sides. Just like that, a little workout turned into a battle.

Sam wasn't allowed to pitch, since he was starting the next day, so Justin and Barry were the pitchers. Luckily for their side, Sam had made Kyle his first pick. When Coach called the game after Dennis got hit, Sam's side was ahead 5–2.

Showering up, Dennis got a look at the red welt on his chest for the first time. Even the guys who just looked at it said "ouch." It was a doozy. Everyone asked how it happened, but Dennis didn't tell anyone until he and Justin were bicycling home. Justin listened in disbelief.

"Are you sure?"

"Believe me," Dennis said. "I wouldn't say anything if I had any doubt. The ball wasn't tricky or hard to handle. It was an easy chance. And even if I had some doubts at first, when I saw that crummy grin on his face afterward I knew for sure."

"Maybe it was just Duane. Maybe Barry didn't know he would do that."

"That's true. That could be."

They rode on while Justin thought it over.

"So why didn't you say anything?" he asked.

"I wanted to. I wanted to punch Duane's lights out," Dennis said. "But I've been trying so hard not to fight with those guys, you know? So when it happened, and after, I just couldn't say anything."

Talking with Justin, Dennis figured out why he hadn't said anything before. Duane had played a stupid trick and by ignoring it, Dennis was coming out ahead. There was only one problem. Dennis wanted to keep the peace, and maybe ignoring Duane was just asking for more trouble. Dennis was tired of all this worrying. He wished they could just start the season over again. They had good players. But how could they start winning games unless they quit beating up on each other?

The next day the team gathered at school for the bus ride to Williamsport. It was their first real travel, since their only away game had been across town at Lincoln Junior High. Williamsport was supposed to have a good team, but Dennis thought today might just be the day to turn the season around. It was a beautiful, sunny day.

As Dennis waited to board the bus, he found himself next to Barry and Duane. He nodded hello.

"Morning."

"Well, good morning, Charlie Hustle," Barry smiled.

So that was what "Charlie" meant. Those guys had been calling him that for a week now. Dennis knew they meant it as an insult. He knew they meant he was an apple-polisher, the kind of guy who gave 110 percent in practice just to impress the coach. He didn't care. He didn't know any other way to play the game. Let them think what they wanted.

"How's your chest?" Duane asked. Dennis just smiled. He could play this game.

"It's okay," he said. "Fix that hole in your glove yet?"

Their turn came to climb aboard. Barry and Duane's pals had claimed the back of the bus, so Dennis found all his friends toward the front with Coach Lanigan. The trip got underway and after a few minutes, Coach stood up. He kept his balance by holding a seat and got everyone's attention.

"I want you all to know that I'm not blind," he began. "I know exactly what's going on." He let it sink in.

"I'm not going to tell you guys that you have to be best friends," Coach continued. "But I don't like the way things are going. Don't look surprised. It's

49

obvious we've got two groups. I'm not going to name names, I don't need to. I just want you to put the team first. You can have your squabbles and rivalries in school or wherever. When it comes to baseball, there's no room for it. 'Nuf said."

Everyone listened, but Dennis wasn't sure it would make any difference.

They arrived at Williamsport ahead of schedule and had plenty of practice time. It was still warm and sunny. A great day for baseball and a great day for Sam McCaskill.

Sam pitched a gem. Williamsport was one of the better teams, but they looked like Little Leaguers today. Luckily, their best pitcher, Matthew Nardizzi, wasn't starting.

In the fifth inning Williamsport scored twice on an error and a pair of singles, but that was all they could manage as Sam collected strikeout victims. Meanwhile, Kyle led the offense, going 3–4 with a triple. Dennis walked and scored his first time up, but struck out in the fourth inning and in his final at bat he got caught trying to stretch a single into a double. Sam and Alan collected RBIs and the final score was Alden 4, Williamsport 2. At last, the Panthers had chalked one up in the win column.

8

For now, they were back on a winning track. Dennis hoped that the team had turned the corner. Maybe the win was all they needed to forget their differences and play ball.

In fact, the game had exactly the opposite effect. Despite Lanigan's lecture, the win had made the players bolder, wilder, more confident. They figured they could go wild and still win. For the next week the Alden Panthers' locker room became a battlefield.

The fake statistics were Justin's idea. It seemed harmless enough. They got a hold of some Alden Athletic Department stationery and typed up the players' batting averages, RBIs and stuff. Naturally, Dennis, Sam, Nick, and Justin—according to these made-up figures—led the team in batting. Barry, Duane, and the rest were way down the list.

Dennis walked by while Larry Stiles was looking at the chart.

"Don't worry, Larry, you'll get that average up."

"Aren't we clever, Charlie," Larry said.

Dennis just smiled, but that "Charlie" business was beginning to bug him.

Then Larry tore the sheet off the wall and ripped it up.

"Oh you're tough, Larry," Dennis said.

"Want to make something of it?"

"No I don't. Why don't you get a sense of humor?"

On Tuesday Sam missed the first half-hour of practice.

"Where've you been, Sam?" Dennis asked as Sam jogged out onto the field.

"Don't ask."

At that, Alan Broadstreet ran by, laughing.

"Sorry, Sam, guess we made a mistake."

"What's going on?" Dennis asked.

"Alan and Brad pulled one over on me," Sam admitted. "I'm heading out and I see them getting on a bus, right? So I asked why they're not going to practice and they said it was cancelled. Like a dork, I get on my own bus home."

"You jerk."

"You said it. Of course on the way out, the bus goes right by the field and I see practice is starting! I got off at the first stop—all the way in Nevins Heights—and jogged all the way back."

Wednesday, Alden played St. Stephens, a small, private school that didn't have very good teams in any of the major team sports. Baseball was no exception.

Barry's turn came in the pitching rotation. He got into quick trouble, giving up two walks and a single to allow one run in the first inning, but after that he was in complete control. He only gave up two more hits in the whole game.

Since the season opener, Barry hadn't tried to throw any more curveballs. In fact, he hardly ever shook off any of Dennis's signs, which surprised Dennis. Barry seemed to realize that it was important to get with his catcher, at least on game days. He still called Dennis "Charlie" whenever he came to the mound, but he would take a piece of advice about pitch location. They had an unspoken truce that only applied during the game.

Alden scored three runs in the first inning and two more in the second. After that, Coach Lanigan began to put in substitutes. It was a good opportunity to give playing time to the second stringers. Barry, who pitched the whole game, was the offensive star as well, collecting three hits for the afternoon. Dennis went 2–3 before Paul Dominick came in to catch the last three innings. The final score was 8–1.

After their terrible start, the Panthers had climbed back to a record of 2–2–1. If they could keep on a roll they might even get back into the division race. After all, they were the only team that had beaten Williamsport so far, and Williamsport and Bradley were tied for first with 4–1 records.

But there was trouble brewing. The locker-room pranks kept going back and forth, getting more and more outrageous. Tempers were beginning to flare.

"You know what they say," Nick suggested. "Don't get mad, get even."

"I guess you're right," Dennis nodded.

Dennis, Sam, and Nick were walking to science class together. Yesterday someone stuck a wad of gum in Justin's cap. By the time he noticed, it was too late. The gum was stuck firmly into his hair. His mother later tried to freeze it with ice and crack it off, but most of it had to be cut out.

"We better not put another bucket of water up, though," Sam said.

"No kidding," Dennis said. "I didn't think about how heavy it was. I figured it would just get him all wet."

"A mistake," Nick agreed.

The heavy plastic bucket had raised a bump on Alan Broadstreet's head, as well as soaked his clothes and notebooks. It was just another step in the wrong direction.

The pranks went back and forth, and weren't very funny. But funny wasn't the main motivation any more. They each wanted revenge.

On Friday after practice Duane yelled, "All right, who's got my glove?"

"What kind of glove? Ski glove?" Nick asked. The guys around snickered.

"Funnyman. I want it now."

No one was admitting they had it. Everyone kept dressing while Duane looked around. It was late, so people were already leaving. Duane was beginning to get mad.

As Nick walked out with his duffel bag, he couldn't resist teasing.

"Duane," he said sincerely, pretending to help, "did you look in your locker? Maybe it's just under a T-shirt or . . ."

He didn't have a chance to finish his sentence because Duane grabbed him by the shirt and slammed him against the side of the lockers.

"Tell me where it is!"

"Take it easy! I really don't know! Cripes!"

Duane let him go.

"You'd better not."

A little while later, Dennis and Justin were waiting outside for their ride home. Mr. Johnson was going to pick them up. Almost everyone had left when Duane stormed by them. Bob Donovan was waiting for Duane nearby. Dennis and Justin could hear them.

"Did you find it, Duane?" asked Bob.

"No. Somebody has it. I'll find it tomorrow," Duane said and they walked off.

Suddenly, Dennis ran back to the gym, but found the doors locked. He gave the handle a tug and then peered in the glass to see if anyone was there. But it was closed up tight. He returned to Justin.

"I've made a big mistake," he said.

"You took it?" asked Justin.

Dennis nodded yes.

"Big deal, that's no mistake. Putting gum in my hair, now *that* was going too far."

"Taking it wasn't the mistake."

"Where is it?"

"You're not going to believe it. The second I did it, I knew it *was* a mistake, but I didn't think it would get left overnight. Oh man. That glove is history."

"Well, where is it?"

"In a toilet."

9

The next day was the South Colby game, to be played at Alden. Dennis made sure he was the first one there.

All night he had tried to figure out what he should do. He talked to Justin and Sam on the phone, but no one saw any perfect way out. Dennis decided he would just have to tell Duane, replace the glove and hope that Coach Lanigan wouldn't find out.

He found the glove where he had left it, but by now it was completely waterlogged. Dennis held it up by two fingers and looked at it hopelessly. He had once left a glove out in the rain. It took a month before it dried out, and it was never the same again anyway. He tried to squeeze some water out of Duane's glove, but it was useless. He gave up, hung it up by his locker and waited.

He began to feel okay about it. Sure it had been stupid thing to do, but now he was taking responsibility for his mistake. He had thirty-five dollars with him—all he had—to give Duane to buy a new glove. He was going to be a man about it. Not like the guy who put the gum in Justin's cap. No one had owned up to that cheap trick yet.

Just then Duane walked by, without saying anything, and without noticing the glove.

Dennis stood up and called Duane's name. The first baseman turned, looking suspicious when he saw that it was Dennis.

"Yeah?"

"I've gotta tell you something."

"I'm listening."

"Come here . . . I've . . . I've got your glove."

Duane walked over slowly, still careful, still expecting a prank.

"So," Duane said. "Old goody-goody Charlie Hustle took my glove, huh?"

"I took it and I'm sorry."

Just then Duane saw the glove, and could see immediately that it was sopping.

"What the . . .?"

"It's wet, soaked," Dennis said, "and probably ruined. I dropped it in a toilet."

Duane shook his head slowly. "You're going to be sorry you did this."

"Before you try to pound my face into the ground, take this," Dennis said, handing him the cash. "I ruined your glove and I'm sorry. That's to replace it. If it's not enough, I'll get more. And I know it was a crummy thing to do."

Duane didn't know quite what to make of Dennis's attitude.

"Yeah, well. What glove do you expect me to play with *today?*"

"I, uh, can't you borrow . . ."

Dennis suddenly realized that he hadn't solved the problem at all. The soaking mitt hanging on the locker was a left-handed first baseman's glove. Pete Phillips and Tim Lopatt were the only other lefties on the team and neither played first.

"I don't know," stuttered Dennis, trying to think of some solution. Duane really had Dennis on the ropes and he knew it.

"Even if I got a new glove today it wouldn't be worn in right for two weeks."

Dennis was stumped. He had thought that everything might work out, but right now he was feeling a whole lot like a jerk.

"Guess I'll have to figure it out myself," Duane said, turning to walk away.

"Don't you want the glove?" Dennis asked. "It'll dry out in a while."

Duane didn't stop walking. He looked back over his shoulder, flashed the money at Dennis and said: "Hey, you bought it, you keep it."

By the time the game started, Dennis had seen that Duane had a regular fielder's glove of his own, besides the first baseman's mitt, and that he could play first perfectly well with it. Still, every time a throw went to first, Dennis thought of the glove and hoped that he wouldn't drop a ball. An error that Duane could blame on the glove would have been a disaster. Luckily, it didn't happen.

Sam was the starting pitcher today. He was really confident in warm-ups, still feeling good after his complete game win over Williamsport. Football had always been his number one sport, and playing quarterback was his dream, but now he was talking about really dedicating himself to pitching. "Maybe

I'll be the next Bo Jackson," he told Dennis. "Pitch in the major leagues and play NFL quarterback as a hobby."

As always, Sam was throwing fastballs. He got South Colby to go three up and three down in the first.

When he returned to the bench, he cracked: "I think I'll throw a no-hitter today."

Dennis noticed that Sam's friends laughed and his enemies didn't. As a matter of fact, the bench was almost exactly divided in half. Barry, Duane, and their friends sat at the far end, while Dennis, Sam, and their loyals sat on the near end. Only Kyle Bushmiller had refused to pick a side. He deliberately sat in a different place every time.

Nick opened the inning with a single and, after Duane popped up, scored on Barry's double to right. It looked like the start of a big inning, but then Kyle and Sam both struck out swinging.

In the top of the second, Sam's first pitch was laced to center for a clean single. Duane chirped: "There goes your no-hitter, McCaskill."

Sam gave up another hit, and got an out on a long fly ball. He fell apart. It was like batting practice for South Colby. After another single Coach Lanigan came out to the mound to talk to Sam. Dennis joined the huddle.

"Don't get rattled here, Sammy," said the Coach. "I want you to show me you can work yourself out of this jam. Move your pitches around more, okay? High and low, high and low."

"Let's get 'em," Dennis said.

Sam walked the next batter, and got the second out on a force out at first. Then he gave up a double and, on the very next pitch, a single. Coach Lanigan came back and pulled the plug. He called Kyle in from left to pitch. Kyle got the next man out, but South had built a 5–1 lead.

The Alden hitters never got into gear. A hit here, a hit there, but no rallies. They just couldn't bunch their hits. Meanwhile, Kyle did okay, allowing two runs over the last five innings, but it was a lost cause. The final was 7–1.

10

Dennis was really let down by the loss to South. Not only had they lost, ending a very short win streak, but he personally had gone 0–3 and hadn't even hit a ball out of the infield. There was only one thing that he was happy about. Apparently, Duane hadn't said anything about the glove to Coach or anyone else. No one had said a word about it. For now, at least, it seemed to be forgotten.

It wasn't.

Monday afternoon at practice, Duane was pitching

while Coach Lanigan was working with some hitters. Dennis was on deck, waiting for Alan to finish hitting. It was taking a while, because Coach was having trouble getting Alan to swing the way he wanted him to.

"No! Look again," Coach said. "Keep the shoulder down, but open your hips. Your hips turn first, see? You're opening up too fast."

Coach's idea was that you got a lot more power in your swing by moving your hips to get your weight into the ball. He was trying to get everyone to do it. It really felt funny at first, to twist like that, and the main mistake everyone made was just what Alan was doing now: twisting his shoulders *before* his hips, instead of keeping his front shoulder down until the swing of the bat carried them open.

Alan took two more swings, missing both, but doing it the way Coach wanted. He didn't look very happy, but Coach Lanigan seemed pleased.

"Okay, Dennis, start hitting a couple to warm up. I'll be right with you," Coach Lanigan said, walking off to show Alan one more thing.

Dennis stepped to the plate, taking a few easy swings to loosen his shoulders. The minute he caught Duane's eye, he knew something was up. But he couldn't quite figure it.

Duane set and pitched. It was on the outside part of the plate, but Dennis swung, hitting a sharp grounder to first.

The next pitch was low, at the knees, but Dennis liked low balls. He went down and got all of it, lifting it deep to center. It banged against the plywood fence.

Dennis had stepped back to watch it and now he took his batting position again, digging his feet in. He watched Duane rear back and fire. Right away, Dennis could see it was inside, very inside, then all at once he realized it was going to hit him!

In that split second, Dennis suddenly knew why Duane had been acting so strangely. Duane was throwing at him on purpose, to get back at him for destroying his glove.

Dennis ducked his head out of the way, twisting to the ground, but the ball banged hard off the back of his batting helmet, and helmet or not, it hurt. It shook him up.

Dennis sat up in the dirt, catching his breath. Coach Lanigan was right there on one knee.

"Are you all right?"

"Yeah, I'm okay," Dennis said. Coach seemed angry and Dennis couldn't figure out why. He was confused. Was it something he had done?

"Where did it hit you? Helmet or head?"

"Just the helmet."

Dennis got up to prove he was okay, and dusted off his pants. Coach sized him up and decided he was all right. Then he turned and walked to the pitcher's mound fast. He was trying to stay somewhat calm, but everyone on the field could hear him.

"You threw at him, didn't you Potter? I'm asking you a question! Did you throw at him? Yes or no?"

Duane didn't back down.

"Yes."

Dennis couldn't believe it. Not that Duane had thrown at him—he *knew* that was true—but that he admitted it. Now Coach Lanigan was *really* mad.

"That was a foolish, dangerous, half-assed move, Potter. Do you know what you did? Do you have an idea what you did?"

Every player on the field and in the dugout was frozen, watching in stunned silence as Coach ranted.

"We're not talking pranks anymore, you little wiseacre punk! If you were my son I'd tan your hide. Get out of here now, Potter," he yelled. "You're history. Gone. You'll never play for this baseball team again."

Duane hadn't moved, hadn't said a word. He just turned and walked slowly off the field.

11

Coach Lanigan meant what he said. Duane Potter was thrown off the team. Lanigan explained his decision in a short meeting after that practice. Brad McCarthy was made the starting first baseman and Tim Lopatt took over Brad's slot in right field.

Dennis didn't know what to think. Like everyone on the team, his first reaction was shock. He thought maybe Coach would let Duane back after his temper cooled.

The rest of practice Monday had been weirdly

quiet. It was so sudden. Duane was here. Then he was gone. There were no wisecracks or pranks in the locker room that afternoon. The guys just dressed and left.

Dennis and Justin got a ride home together from Dennis's mom. On the drive, they talked it over.

"I don't think it was fair," said Dennis. "Basically, he did one thing wrong, you know? He had no warning."

"Yeah, but he threw that ball at your head," Justin said. "That's crazy."

"I agree," Mrs. Clements said.

"Of course a *Mom* would think that," Dennis teased.

"Anyone would," she said. "You just can't go around hurting people with something as dangerous as a hardball."

"But major league pitchers throw at batters all the time," Dennis said.

"Well, they shouldn't."

"It is against the rules," Justin said. "And people have been badly hurt that way."

"It just wasn't that big a deal. It was just a gag, a prank," Dennis said.

"You mean like taking someone's glove." Justin smiled at Dennis. Justin knew that Mrs. Clements didn't know. Dennis gave him a look that said, "Say anything and I'll tapdance on your face."

"Yeah, just like taking someone's glove," Dennis said. "Just a simple, harmless thing."

"What are you boys talking about?" Mrs. Clements asked.

"Nothing, Mom," Dennis said, and he changed the subject.

That night Dennis decided that Coach Lanigan would change his mind. He had to. In a way, Dennis felt responsible. If he hadn't ruined Duane's glove, Duane wouldn't have thrown that baseball. Dennis had an even worse thought. Duane would probably go to Coach Lanigan and tell him about the glove now, to explain why he had thrown the ball, why he was so angry. Dennis groaned to himself. Lanigan wouldn't kick *him* off the team, too, would he? Dennis kept thinking and worrying about it, but he finally convinced himself that somehow things would work out.

Dennis was anxious to find out what Kyle thought. The feud was still on, Duane or no Duane. Dennis was afraid that he would be driven to the other side by Coach Lanigan's harsh treatment of Duane. Sam and Dennis talked to Kyle as the team walked out to the practice field.

"Hey, Kyle," Dennis said.

"Hey, guys."

"What's going on."

"Not much."

Kyle was a great hitter, but he wasn't much of a talker.

"So, what do you think about Duane?" Sam asked.

"It's too bad," Kyle said. "But you mess up, you pay the price."

Dennis was surprised, but glad. At least Kyle wasn't going to join the other guys.

"By the way," Kyle said, "that doesn't mean I'm going to get involved in this stupid rivalry thing, okay? I just want to play ball, so leave me out of it."

Sam and Dennis didn't have any response to that. So they walked the rest of the way to the field in silence.

Practice that day was quieter than the day before. Coach Lanigan knew that his decision wasn't popular, but he wasn't giving an inch. Duane's friends were rude to him, ignoring his comments and suggestions, barely listening to his directions. Dennis saw him take a couple of the players aside and talk to them in a serious way.

The other group of players wasn't much happier. Sam and Nick said they were glad that Duane was gone, and that he definitely deserved it. The three of them talked it over after practice while they waited for their rides.

"Look, I'm glad for the support," Dennis said, "but I'm not sure it's as simple as taking sides."

"What do you mean?" Sam asked.

"Well, we've been fighting back and forth for weeks, and then there was Duane's glove."

"So? None of that was as bad as throwing at you," Nick said.

"I'm just thinking that Coach might be playing favorites a little. Do you think he would have thrown Sam off the team for the same thing?"

Sam and Nick thought it over. Dennis had a point.

"But who cares?" Nick said. "At least we get rid of Duane."

"Yeah, but that could backfire," Sam pointed out. "Everyone will turn against us because it'll seem like our fault."

Sam and Nick's ride arrived, so they grabbed their bags and left. Dennis thought it over but he couldn't come up with any good answer. He just hoped that Duane's friends would see that the whole mess wasn't his fault.

The next day was a road trip to Bradley. It was a half-hour trip and the first time all year the players actually did homework on the bus. Why not? It was as quiet as a library.

Barry pitched a great game, but Alden couldn't put the round bats on the round ball. An unearned run came around in the fourth inning for Bradley, on an error, a sacrifice bunt, and a single. Kyle collected three hits, but never had any runners to drive in. Alden failed to score. Bradley added one more run in the bottom of the sixth, and it was all they needed. Bradley won, 2–0, and Alden's record fell to 2–4–1.

12

The loss to Bradley didn't get the Alden Panthers baseball team down. How could it? They were at rock bottom before they even played. Barry's great pitching had kept it close, but in fact, they never had a chance. They expected to lose, so they did.

Dennis was frustrated. The more he tried to concentrate on playing baseball, the more distracted he became. He had allowed two Bradley runners to steal second, and again failed to get a hit. His season was falling apart.

Thursday before school, Dennis had an early

morning appointment for a checkup with Dr. Palaver, his dentist. The offices were near Alden, so his mother dropped him off on her way to work. He could walk to school afterward.

The door jingled as he stepped into the reception area. Dennis checked in with the nurse and then turned to find a seat in the waiting area. There, reading a worn-out copy of *Sport* magazine, was Duane Potter. Dennis looked away, pretending he hadn't seen him, but then crossed the room and sat one seat away from his former teammate. He was sure Duane had seen him by now, but Duane was still reading, pretending not to have noticed.

"Uh, hi, Duane."

Duane just looked up and mumbled a reply.

"Checkup?" Dennis asked.

"No," Duane snapped. "I just like waiting rooms."

"Okay, fine. I'm sorry about what Coach did, you know. I thought it was pretty tough."

Duane shrugged.

"Look, I don't mean to bug you, I'll leave in a sec," Dennis said. "But I gotta know—what did you tell Coach Lanigan? Didn't you tell him about the glove and all the pranks and stuff?"

"Nope."

"Nothing?"

"Coach called me up the next day and just gave me a line about what was wrong with me and why he gave me the boot. I just said yeah, thanks, that's all."

"Why didn't you say something? Maybe he would let you back on the team if you told him why you did it."

"I don't want to be back on Lanigan's team. Who needs it?"

"C'mon, why really?"

"If I told him then we both get kicked off the team, we're both in trouble," Duane said. "Maybe I should have done that to get back at you, but I didn't. I guess you owe me a favor."

"Are you serious?"

"Look," Duane said. "I didn't do it as a good deed to you. I just don't like Lanigan and I didn't want to tell him anything. I guess I shouldn't have thrown at you. I wish I hadn't done it but I just wasn't thinking. That's all, case closed. All right?"

The receptionist called Duane's name. He stood up and walked into the office leaving Dennis more confused than before. Why was Duane protecting him from Coach? Was it just because he didn't like Lanigan? Or was it because he was actually sorry about throwing that beanball?

Dennis was called in after a few minutes, had his teeth cleaned, listened to Dr. Palaver's terrible jokes, and was glad to be told he had no cavities. Unfortunately, when he got out he still had plenty of time to get to school before homeroom.

All day, Dennis kept thinking about what Duane had said. He had a study hall right before lunch with Nick and Sam.

"All right, enough about Duane, we've really got to study for this quiz," Sam announced. "Now, let's do the Bill of Rights. What does the Fourth Amendment say?"

"Is that the one about self-discrimination?" Nick asked.

"No, it's the right to bear arms, isn't it?" Dennis said.

"Wrong," Sam sighed. "It's the one about arrest warrants, search and seizure. Didn't you guys study these yet?"

"Yeah, but they're so complicated," Dennis groaned. "We're doomed."

They sat quietly, wondering what to do, then gave up.

"So," Nick said, "do you think Duane will be back?"

"I'll bet he is," Sam said.

"I don't know," Dennis said. "He sounded pretty

angry at Coach Lanigan. Even if Coach allowed him back, I'm not sure he'd play."

"No way," Sam said. "Duane loves baseball. It's his best sport. He'd come back in a second."

"You know, I don't like Duane, I never have and I never will. He's loud, stupid, and generally a pain," Dennis said, "but, you gotta admit he got a raw deal."

"I sure don't miss having him on the team," Nick said.

"At the same time," Dennis continued, "I gotta respect what he did. I mean, he could have pointed the finger at me. Even if it didn't get him out of trouble, at least he might have taken me down with him, but he didn't do it."

"He was just too dumb to think of it," Sam joked.

"I don't know," Dennis said. "And the other thing, the main thing really, is that the team is in deep trouble. We'll never win any games until both sides agree to a truce and try to play together."

"And that'll never happen while Duane is gone," Nick admitted.

"True," Dennis said.

"They blame us for it," Sam said. "But what could we do?"

"Duane did himself in," Nick agreed. "There's nothing we can do about it now."

The three ballplayers soon returned to trying to memorize the Bill of Rights, but in the meantime, Dennis had made a decision. He didn't say anything to his friends about it. He couldn't. But Dennis had made up his mind that something had to be done. And he had to do it alone.

13

"I think," Dennis paused. "I think that Duane deserves a second chance."

Dennis spoke uncertainly, but his mind was made
up. All day long he had hesitated, wondering what
would happen, what he would say. But now, standing
in front of Coach Lanigan, he felt like whatever happened, he was doing the right thing.

Coach Lanigan looked surprised, then he half-
smiled.

"You and Duane aren't exactly friends."

"That's true."

"More like enemies."

Dennis nodded.

"So tell me why you think he deserves to play for our team."

"Well," Dennis gulped, "what he did was wrong, I know, but it wasn't that bad."

Coach Lanigan thought it over, twirling a pencil in his hands. Dennis knew he hadn't quite told the whole truth. He tried again.

"And, uh, I feel like it was partly my fault. You know, we've been fighting and stuff."

Still not quite the truth, but closer. Dennis waited. Coach Lanigan cleared his throat and spoke.

"I didn't kick Duane off the team because he threw at you, Dennis," he said. "I kicked him off because he threw at *anyone*. I just can't excuse that kind of behavior. Now I know that there has been a big rivalry going back and forth on the team. It's obvious. And I'm sure you did something that made Duane real mad, but you don't throw at a batter on purpose. Not on my team. You just don't."

Dennis nodded. So Coach had figured out that Duane was getting revenge. Dennis just hoped he wouldn't ask what the revenge was for.

"Still, I'm glad you came to me. To tell you the truth I was already thinking of asking Duane if he'd like to come back. I'm glad you think he deserves another chance. Maybe it means we can start to get you guys playing as a team."

"Thanks. Um, Coach."

"Yes?"

"Look, don't tell anyone I came and said what I did, okay? Especially not Duane."

"I'll try not to," Coach Lanigan laughed.

Duane was not at practice that afternoon. Dennis wondered if Coach had talked to him yet. Even if he had it was certainly possible that Duane would refuse to come back.

The next day, Dennis saw Duane coming out of Coach's office by the gym. He walked into the locker room and there was Duane, already getting into his uniform. Dennis couldn't help himself, he smiled at him. Duane just looked away. Their conversation at the dentist's was okay, because no one had to know about it, but it was different here; this was the battlefield.

After dressing, Dennis walked to the field with Sam.

"I would never have imagined that seeing Duane Potter would make me so happy," Dennis laughed.

"Have you lost your mind?" Sam responded.

"We've got to cut the crap on this team," Dennis

said. "We were wrong to fight those guys. It doesn't matter whose fault it was. If we tried, we could figure a way to play together as a team."

"Here we go again," Sam said. "The old peace-making act. Those guys just aren't worth it, Dennis."

"They're the only team we've got."

Out on the field, Dennis watched Duane's friends gather around him, excited, slapping him on the back, eager to get the scoop on how he had gotten back. Dennis wondered what he was saying. At least the mood was upbeat, even if it was the same old story with the two sides.

Saturday there was a game at North Colby. It was Sam's turn to start and Alden was looking to win. The first time they had played North the game had ended in a tie. In a way, both games were on the line. Coach Lanigan kept Brad at first base. Duane was going to have to earn his starting slot again.

It was a tight game. After three innings there was no score. Sam was back in form, throwing hard and throwing strikes. Barry made a clutch error at third, overthrowing first, but they got out of the inning when Alan turned a terrific double play. As always, Kyle was hitting the ball hard, but today he couldn't buy a break. He lined out to center and lined out to short.

Two more scoreless innings went by. It was the top of the sixth inning. Larry Stiles was leading off, batting in the number six spot. He hit a grounder that went deep in the hole at short. It looked like an out, but then the North shortstop couldn't get the ball out of his glove. He held the ball and Larry was safe on first with no outs.

Dennis was up next. As he walked to the plate, he watched Coach Lanigan carefully. Coach took off his cap and put it on again—that was the sign to sacrifice. He would try to bunt, to get Larry over to scoring position at second.

He waited on the first pitch. It was a ball. The next one was across and he squared himself and laid the ball down. It was a beauty, but Dennis wasn't wasting any time admiring it. He was charging for first, sacrifice or no sacrifice. You never knew what could happen.

The North third baseman caught the ball and made the mistake of going for Larry at second. He was safe by a mile. Now there were two on and still no outs. Every player on the Alden bench jumped up, forgetting all about who was on which side in the excitement. They all wanted to win.

Alan popped out, too shallow for the runners to advance. Justin started out toward the plate, but

Coach Lanigan called him back. Duane had a bat in his hands. Coach was sending him in to pinch hit for Justin.

As Justin walked in past Duane, he put out a hand, and Duane slapped it.

Duane looked determined to bring in the runs. He took the first two pitches for balls, but he was itching to swing. On the next pitch he took a big swing and fouled it back for strike one. Dennis and Larry took their leads off first and second. The pitcher set and threw. Duane took a mighty cut and this time he caught up with it.

It was long and deep to left, but curving toward foul territory. Dennis watched on his toes, waiting to run. It was fair and over the fence for a home run!

"Yeah!" The Alden bench erupted.

"Dinger!"

"Whoooooweee!"

Dennis was whooping and hollering as he ran the bases. He crossed home, stamping the plate and turned to wait for Duane. A pinch-hit home run! What a hit!

Duane came across the plate grinning from ear to ear.

"Massive shot!" Larry yelled.

"What a blast," Dennis yelped.

Duane slapped both their hands. In a moment he was surrounded in a babble of congratulations: "Clutch!" "Awesome!" "What a ride!"

And among them, Coach Lanigan, who stuck out his hand for Duane to slap: "Welcome back."

14

Duane's three-run homer won the game. Sam polished off a great game, mowing down North Colby batters for the final two innings and collecting a shutout victory, 3–0.

Dennis and Duane had exchanged a low five but it wasn't exactly a peace treaty. Everyone celebrated the home run, but it was clear who was and wasn't welcome in the inner circle around Duane. Even in victory the team was divided. The Panthers were still two teams that just happened to wear the same uniform.

Still, Dennis thought he noticed a change.

"Nick, do you think Duane is kind of, I don't know, acting friendlier."

"No."

The two were waiting outside for homeroom Monday morning.

"Not a big change," Dennis suggested. "Just a little, like, he doesn't seem so angry."

"Sorry, Dennis. I'm afraid it's wishful thinking."

"Think I'm imagining it, huh?"

The morning bell rang and they headed for their separate homerooms. Nick just shrugged his shoulders.

"It would be nice, but I don't see it."

At Monday practices, Coach Lanigan generally let them play a scrimmage game after their warm-ups and drills. He didn't let them pick their own teams anymore though. He knew that was asking for trouble.

This particular Monday, trouble happened anyway.

Dennis came to the plate in the second inning, with Jimmy Carlisle on third and two outs. Kyle was pitching. Dennis worked the count to 2–2, fouled off a couple strikes, and finally slashed a single to right. Jimmy came in to score easily.

Leading off first, with two out and Paul Dominick catching, Dennis decided he would take a chance and try to steal second. He figured it was always a good idea to remind Coach Lanigan that Paul, the backup catcher, didn't have such a good arm. Dennis edged off first.

Kyle threw the first pitch to Dave Zinsser, who took it for ball one. Dennis bluffed toward second, but went back. Kyle noticed. Before his next pitch he threw over to first, to make sure Dennis didn't get too much of a lead. Now Paul also knew that Dennis was a threat to steal. The element of surprise was gone, but Dennis still wanted to run. He knew Paul couldn't get him.

Kyle threw, Dave swung and missed and Dennis held. On the next pitch, Dennis took off. He had a good jump, but half-way to second he stepped on a hole in the rough infield. It was just enough to get him off stride. He almost fell forward, but regained his balance. The near-trip had cost him valuable time, though. He slid into second head first, but Barry took the throw in plenty of time to make the tag—and he made it, with a little something extra. Instead of just laying the tag on him, Barry slapped it on as hard as he could. To Dennis it felt like a hard punch on the shoulder, one that glanced off and caught him on the side of the head, too.

"You're a cheapshot artist, Sanderson!" Dennis barked in anger.

Barry played innocent, giving Dennis a "who, me?" look and then smiled and turned away. Dennis was mad. He forgot all about the peacemaking rap. He wouldn't forget this. He would get even sooner or later.

His chance came sooner.

Two innings later, Dennis again reached first, this time on a walk. There was one out and Dave hit a slow grounder to second. Watching the play as he ran, Dennis knew it could be a double play, but it would be close. Dennis's job was to break up that double play, by sliding into the pivot man at second. Dennis would do this job with pleasure.

Mitch Tompkins fielded the ball cleanly and threw to Barry to get the force at second. As Barry tried to make the throw to first, Dennis hit him hard. Barry nearly flipped as Dennis cut his legs out from under him. It was a tough play, but within the rules.

Barry didn't care. He came up swinging. Dennis wasn't surprised and the two quickly tumbled to the ground in a flurry of punches. Everyone ran to join the battle. Mitch was moving in when Sam jumped on his back and they began to wrestle. Duane, running in from first, was one of the first to arrive, but instead of joining the scuffle, he jumped in between Dennis and Barry, trying to break it up.

"Cool it! Cut it out!" Duane yelled. He got hold of Barry, but by doing that, he let Dennis's last punch get through, a solid right to Barry's cheek.

Justin was also trying to break up the fight and Dennis and Barry were separated by the time Coach Lanigan arrived. Sam had thrown Mitch off him and their fight petered out.

"Thanks a lot!" Barry yelled at Duane, twisting himself angrily out of his friend's grasp.

"I was just trying to stop . . ." Duane began.

Barry shoved Duane in the chest with both hands. He was angry at Duane for allowing him to get hit. The other smaller fights had broken up by now.

"That's *enough!*" Coach stormed. Everyone shut up. They could tell he was really mad.

"I don't know what's wrong with you guys," he said. "You'd rather beat up on each other than play baseball."

Things calmed down. Coach made Dennis and Barry shake hands and called the game. Barry's eye was already getting black. They returned to practice as usual.

Watching Duane play peacemaker, Dennis was convinced that he had changed. But why? He had to find out. Maybe whatever had made him change could make the others change, too. Maybe if Duane would loosen up, they could get the rest to follow. Maybe, just maybe, this team could still put aside their differences and get down to the business of playing ball. But they had better do it soon. There wasn't all that much season left.

15

"I just want to ask one question," Dennis said as he waited by Duane's locker the next day. "Why did you try to break up the fight, instead of jumping in?"

Duane thought it over as he opened his locker.

"I guess I wanted you to get a free shot at Barry's nose."

"C'mon, really."

"You want to know, huh? All right. Two things. One, while I was kicked off the team I realized what a waste all the fighting was."

He paused.

"What's the other thing?"

"Coach Lanigan told me what you did—told me you asked him to give me another chance."

Dennis was surprised.

"I told him not to say anything."

"Well he did," Duane said. "Don't worry, I didn't tell anyone else."

"Don't."

"Fine. Anyway, it was decent of you, but the main point is that this team isn't going anywhere so long as we keep knocking each other down."

"We should all do what Kyle does, just play ball."

"Look," Duane said. "This peace pow-wow stuff is stupid, but we've got to do something, right? So I'll try to get the message to my side and you work on the wimps, okay?"

"My friends weren't the problem in the first place," Dennis said. "So if the 'Moron Club' will cut the crap then we will, too."

"Deal," Duane said. Dennis started to leave.

"Hey, Charlie Hustle," Duane called.

"What?" Dennis asked.

"I still think you're a brown-nosing dink," Duane said, but he was smiling. Dennis grinned back and said:

"And I still think that you're as dumb as a board."

With that Dennis headed off to homeroom. He was psyched. He didn't know how much all this could really do to help the team, but he knew it couldn't hurt. They were playing a tough game tomorrow, against Williamsport. They had beaten Williamsport in their first meeting, but they hadn't faced their best pitcher, a kid named Matthew Nardizzi. They had heard all about this guy from other teams. He was supposed to be incredible, the best pitcher in the league. Nardizzi's record was nothing to sneeze at: two no-hitters and five wins in five games.

But Nardizzi could have been Dwight Gooden, for all Dennis cared. He was convinced that the new Alden Panthers could beat anybody. He passed the word around to his friends that there was a cease-fire. At Tuesday practice he thought he could already tell that the split was getting better. It was nothing major, just little things: Larry picking up a ball for Sam, Mitch and Nick warming up together, a wise-crack that the whole team laughed at. Dennis watched it all happening and didn't see how they could lose.

Maybe that was because he hadn't seen Matthew Nardizzi pitch yet.

Even during his warm-ups, Nardizzi was impressive. The Panthers watched, listening to the loud whap as his pitches smacked into the catcher's glove.

"Check it out," Sam said quietly to Dennis.

"No kidding."

"How does such a little guy throw so hard?" Justin wondered.

"Bullets," Dennis agreed.

"Right where he wants 'em, too," Justin said.

"We can hit him," Dennis said. "We've just gotta get around on him. Wrists, boys, quick wrists."

The boys from Alden battled, but they might as well have been swinging toothpicks. Nardizzi mowed them down. Still, Alden kept it close as Barry pitched well, and the team played good defense. Kyle made a radical running catch in left field and Sam turned a great double play to get out of a jam in the second inning. It didn't last, though. In the third, Barry gave up a single and a home run and Williamsport jumped to a 2–0 lead.

In the bottom of the third, Dennis led off. He had been watching Nardizzi carefully, trying to get a sense of how to time him. He had noticed that everyone was undercutting the pitches, hitting a lot of fly balls. He was determined not to make the same mistake.

Dennis was ready to swing, but the first pitch was so fast he just watched. The umpire called it a strike. Dennis stepped back out. He had to be *ready*.

The pitch was high, but he swung, fouling it off into the backstop for the second strike. Nardizzi could flat out throw! Dennis inched his hands up the bat. By choking up, he hoped to make his swing quicker. He reminded himself not to swing under the pitch.

On the next pitch Dennis swung. He got good wood on the ball, but he hit it down, a grounder to short where it was fielded cleanly and relayed to first for an easy out. Dennis returned to the bench, as frustrated as the rest. Justin was up next, and he finally got the first hit for Alden, a blooper just out of the second baseman's reach. But they failed to score.

The visitors scored another run in the top of the sixth. On their third trip to the plate, when some of the Alden batters were finally starting to catch up to Nardizzi's fastball, he bamboozled them by mixing in a wicked change-of-pace pitch. The final was Williamsport 3, Alden 0.

After the game, Coach tried to buck up his squad.

"I liked your effort today," he began, and there were moans from throughout the bus.

"No, I'm serious. I saw good concentration from every batter."

"That's, cause we were scared of getting hit," Nick cracked, and everyone laughed.

"Okay, okay. You guys should feel okay though. You came across a good pitcher on a great day. Some of the other losses have been tough to take, but today we did our job. You took your best shots and you should be proud."

16

"I still say baseball is a game of individuals," Justin stated firmly, laying down his fork.

It was the usual lunch table crowd, one-half of the team: Justin, Dennis, Sam, Nick, Dave, Jimmy, and some others. Naturally, they were talking baseball.

"No way," Dennis said, munching a corn chip. "Maybe you're basically on your own at the plate, but you've got to be part of a team. You've got to know that the guys on the bench are rooting for you."

"I agree. I used to think Justin was right," Sam said, "but we waste an awful lot of time in practice fighting and ragging on people. If we got along, we'd get a lot more done."

Nick laughed: "Maybe we should all hold hands during practice."

"Or give each other lollipops," Dave suggested.

"Very funny," Sam said. "I guess you guys like being 3–5–1."

"We're better than that," Dennis said. "We just have to quit fighting."

Dennis wondered if Duane and his friends ever had conversations like this. He doubted it. Still, he hoped that Duane could get the idea across that the team had to change. It may have been too late to have a great season this year, but the same guys would be back next year, and the year after. They had to find some way to get along. The sooner the better.

Thursday and Friday at practice, Dennis looked for signs of improvement. There wasn't much he could put his finger on, but things seemed better, or at least calmer. He did his best to be friendly to the "enemies." In fact, he was even getting used to being called Charlie Hustle. Why complain? If it was a good enough nickname for Pete Rose, it was sure good enough for Dennis Clements.

Saturday, St. Stephens came to town, bringing

their 0–8 record with them. It was more like an extra practice than a game.

The Alden hitters jumped all over the St. Stephens pitcher, scoring four runs in the first and two more in the second before the first relief pitcher came in. After Williamsport, this was like taking candy from a baby.

Sam was getting them out with ease. Coach Lanigan again used the opportunity to play his substitutes. But even the Alden second-stringers were better than the competition. Sam gave up a few hits, but didn't let them score. The final was a football score, Alden 13–0.

St. Stephens had been no test, and Dennis knew it. They wouldn't have to wait long for a challenge, though. The next Wednesday they would travel to South Colby, hoping to avenge their earlier 7–1 defeat.

Monday, Coach, who had noticed the improved attitude, let them play a scrimmage game. In the third inning or so, with Barry pitching, Sam came up. While he was getting ready to hit, he teased Dennis, who was catching.

"If I get on, I'm going to steal on your no-good arm."

"You just try it, my slow-footed friend."

On the second pitch, Sam slapped a single into center field. After the first pitch to the next batter, Dennis walked out to the mound, and on his way, called Duane over from first.

Both Barry and Duane looked a little surprised. Dennis didn't come out too often when Barry was pitching, and why would he need to talk to Duane? It wasn't like there was a bunting situation or anything. It only took three whispered words for them to understand.

"Hidden ball trick," Dennis said, working hard not to smile.

Barry and Duane looked at him in surprise. Pulling the hidden ball trick on his own pal Sam? They tried to keep straight faces, too, but Dennis could tell they liked the idea. They pretended to talk and Dennis slipped the ball to Duane, and pretended to give it to Barry. Dennis glanced at Sam. He wasn't paying attention. They returned to their positions.

Dennis crouched down and gave the signals. Barry looked in, nodded, set himself—looking just like he was about to pitch.

Sam went for it hook, line, and sinker.

He took two steps off first and Duane tagged him, plucking the ball out of his glove and showing it to him triumphantly. Sam was dumbstruck. Then he just rolled his eyes and walked off the field. On his way he pointed at Dennis.

"Somehow, I know that was your idea," he yelled.

Dennis smiled at him.

"Just keeping you on your toes."

Dennis was glad the trick play had worked. It was all in good fun, for a change, and would keep the team loose.

Wednesday came and the mood on the team was good. It felt like they were starting over, even though they were down to their last two games. After South Colby, Alden would play their final game against Lincoln Junior High, next Saturday. Right now their record was 4–5–1. If they could win these last couple they would actually end up with a winning record.

If there had been announcers, they would have called it a great day for baseball. It was warm and sunny, with a refreshing breeze blowing across the South Colby field.

Alden jumped out to a first inning lead as Nick singled and Kyle drove him home with a long double. Barry went after the hitters and got them three up and three down. It looked like it just might be Alden's day.

"Yes! Barry!"

"Down in order."

"Let's pile it on! Keep after 'em!"

Alden scored again in the third, as Kyle singled and stole second, coming home on Larry's single. In the bottom of the third, Barry ran into trouble. After giving up a single and a walk, he got the next batter to hit a ground ball to short. It looked like a sure double play, but Alan was in such a hurry to make the play that he totally botched it. The ball skipped off the tip of his glove into center.

The runner from second came around to score and instead of two outs, there were still none out, and there were two on. Barry was really upset. He stomped around the mound, slapping his glove. He didn't say anything to Alan, but his behavior said it all. Alan hung his head. It was a dumb mistake. Barry started to pitch again, but he was all steamed up. He walked the next batter to load up the bases and Coach Lanigan came out to calm him down. While they talked, Dennis looked out at Alan. He wished he could say something to him. He looked so shaky and nervous after his error.

Coach left Barry in. The next batter hit an easy grounder to Alan at short. Dennis held his breath, but sure enough, Alan bobbled it. He managed to get it over to Justin at second for the force, but it could have been a double play. Since it wasn't, another run scored. Now the game was tied 2–2.

Barry was fuming. He walked the next batter to load the bases again. Coach came out and took the ball, calling on Duane to take over. Duane threw smoke, striking out the first batter he faced, and then getting a pop fly to end the inning.

Duane and the opposing pitcher settled into a duel over the next three innings. South scored a run, but Alden came right back to tie it up.

It was still 3–3 when Dennis stepped to the plate in the top of the seventh. There were two outs, but Sam and Larry were on the corners. It was hero time, and Dennis was ready.

South's pitcher was getting tired. His fastball was losing its zip, but he was getting them out with a smart mix of locations. Dennis just wanted to make sure to wait on the ball. He concentrated on seeing the ball before he swung.

The first two pitches were balls. Dennis figured he would gladly take a walk, load up the bases for Alan. But the next pitch was a called strike and then he fouled one off for strike two. Now he had to protect the plate. The next pitch was down at the knees— right where Dennis liked it. He knew even as he swung that he was going to get it. The ball was hit on a line, over the leaping shortstop's glove, and Sam rounded third and scored. Alden had the lead again. Alan grounded out, but at least now South *had* to score.

And they didn't. Duane smelled the victory and really went after them. He struck out two and Larry, playing third, made a swell catch for the final out. Alden won 4–3 and they were back to .500 with a record of 5–5–1.

The locker room was a new place. No one was looking over his shoulder for flying shampoo, or broom booby traps.

Barry dropped a ball that rolled into the aisle. Justin picked it up.

"Here you go, Ace," Justin said with a toss.

"Thanks."

"Nice game, Potter," Dennis said as Duane walked by.

"You too, Clements."

Everyone was making an effort. It was a little strained but at least they were all on the same side, the winning side. It was like starting over.

17

Even Justin was convinced. Alden had played as a team, and they had played their best game of the season. It may have gone against logic, but it was impossible to deny.

The guys talked about it over pizza on Friday night. It was Sam's thirteenth birthday. He had decided he was too old for a party, but he had asked his dad to take him and his friends out for pizza.

While the others munched, Dennis explained his philosophy of baseball.

"It's what the sportscasters call the 'intangibles,' " Dennis began.

"What's an 'intangible'?" Sam asked.

"It's something you can't touch," Nick said.

"That doesn't make any sense," Sam said.

"Well, in baseball," Dennis explained, though he wasn't quite sure himself, "I guess it means the little things that don't show up in the box score, you know? Sharp defense, a winning attitude, that kind of stuff."

"Right," Justin said, "and they *shouldn't* really make a big difference. . . ."

"Justin! We've already been through . . ." Dennis started to say.

"But I guess sometimes they do," Justin said with a laugh.

"Right," Nick piped in. "Great team attitude like when Barry got so angry at Alan."

"But that just proves the point," Dennis said. "Barry got so upset that he blew himself out of the game. If he had acted like the error was no big deal, well, it could have changed everything. Alan could have played better, Barry could have pitched better. . . . Luckily it all worked out anyway."

"I heard that Barry apologized to Alan," Sam said.

"Yeah, I heard that," Nick said.

"Anyway," Dennis went on, "the point is we've got a much better team than our record shows, because we were held back by all the fights."

"All the intangibles," Nick said.

"Yeah, *bad* intangibles," Dennis said.

"And now we have good intangibles?" Justin asked.

"Right."

"So that's why we can beat Lincoln?" Justin asked.

"But we lost so badly to Lincoln the first time," Sam said.

"Yeah, 11–4," Justin agreed.

"Doesn't matter a bit," Dennis said. "I personally *guarantee* a victory."

The guys pretended to be impressed by the boldness of Dennis's statement but they knew he was half-kidding. At the same time, that meant he was half-serious. Game time was only a good night's sleep away and Dennis was getting them up for the game. It was too late to change the whole season, but somehow this one meant a lot. They wanted to end up on the plus side, and the game was against their crosstown rival. They knew a lot of the Lincoln kids from around town. They were playing for local bragging rights.

Saturday was another great day for baseball. The

early morning cloud cover had blown away, leaving only a few high clouds scattered against the blue sky. Dennis could smell summer in the air. He was ready to play.

The whole Alden team began the game with high hopes, but though the sun kept shining, the team's spirits grew quickly dark. Sam didn't have it today, nor did Kyle, who came in to relieve. It seemed that Lincoln's first inning would never end, and when it finally did, seven runs had scored.

Seven to zero in the bottom of the first. It was a disaster. The Alden players were stunned. All their preparations, the extra efforts, the new attitude, all of it was crushed under the weight of those seven runs. The dugout was quiet, not hopeless yet, but pretty close.

The Lincoln pitcher walked Nick to open the game, but got the next three out, including Kyle, who grounded weakly to first. In the top of the second Kyle's pitching was fading fast. He gave up two singles and Coach Lanigan moved him back to left, bringing Justin in to pitch.

Justin, the third Panther pitcher, finally began to get the game under control. Mixing his pitches well, he retired the first three batters he faced. Alden did nothing in their half-inning, but Justin again retired

Lincoln in order. At least Lincoln wasn't getting any farther ahead. The mood in the dugout was grim. Everyone was doing their best not to give up, but it was tough with the scoreboard staring you in the face: 7–0. Dennis tried to keep up the chatter. This would be a real test of the team's character. Could they keep hustling and scrapping even when they were in the hole seven runs?

In the third inning, Alden got a little rally going. Nick and Duane each singled and then Barry reached on a Lincoln error. The bases were loaded for Kyle, who came through with a clutch single to score two runs. Mitch walked to load the bases again. Just as Alden's hopes were rising, Lincoln turned a nifty twin killing to end the uprising.

Justin was pitching the best game of his young career. He gave up a hit in the fourth, but again kept Lincoln from scoring. He wasn't overpowering—he just got the outs he needed. Alden added another run in the bottom of the inning. Alan singled and stole second, then reached third on an overthrow. Dennis brought him home with a deep sacrifice fly. Slowly, Dennis and the other Panthers were starting to believe again. One run at a time, they were closing in. It was 7–3, but maybe they *could* come back. If Justin could hold Lincoln, and if they could just get a few hits at the right time, but those were big "ifs."

In the fifth inning, Justin gave up a single and a walk. But a sure run was saved when Barry made a miracle snare of a line drive at third. As if that wasn't enough, Sam made a great heads-up play at short to get the last out.

The breaks were starting to go Alden's way. But Dennis wondered if it was too late. They were still down four runs. They made three outs in order in the fifth. Now they only had two innings left.

Dennis returned to the field with Justin. In the warmth, Justin was sweating. He pulled off his cap and pushed back his straight dark hair, then put on his cap again.

"Don't work too hard, Justin," Dennis encouraged. "You're on today, just befuddle 'em around the corners."

Justin did just that, to keep them within shooting distance by again posting a bagel on the scoreboard.

Then Alden lit up again. Kyle led off with a triple, and scored when the next pitch was wild, skipping off to the backstop. Mitch looped a double over the first baseman's head. Alan struck out, but then Dennis and Brad both singled. It was 7–5, with just one out and men at first and third. Justin was at the plate.

"Wait for your pitch!" Sam yelled.

"Get your cut, get your cut!" Duane cheered.

After taking two pitches, Justin hit a grounder to third. Figuring that they would try to go to second to make the double play, Dennis tore for home. The Lincoln third baseman fielded the ball cleanly, but double-clutched when he saw Dennis run. Instead of going to second, as he should have, he turned and threw to the catcher.

It was a bad throw up the line, and the catcher had to come out to get it. The ball and Dennis arrived at the same time. Dennis steamrolled the Lincoln catcher, who entirely missed the ball. Dennis tagged the plate and meanwhile Justin and Brad advanced to second and third.

Just like that it was a one-run game. Nick grounded out, but Brad scored on the play and it was tied up. Duane gave the ball a ride, as the Panthers held their breath, but the Lincoln center fielder made a great running grab to end the inning.

Alden took the field with a roar, slapping gloves, bearing down to win this game.

"We're back, all the way back!" Dennis yelled.

"Let's get 'em, now," Barry added. "Let's nail 'em."

No one in the dugout was sitting, and they hadn't been for the last two innings.

But Justin was tiring. He walked the first batter. He got the next man to pop up, but after falling behind 3–0, gave up a single to left. Luckily the runner had to hold at second. Justin threw his next pitch wide and in the dirt, but Dennis leaped out to block it. Justin walked the batter and Coach Lanigan made the slow walk to the mound. Now Duane got the call. One out. Bases loaded.

After warming up, Duane set to work. His first two pitches were called balls. Dennis walked the ball back to the mound.

"Just throw it hard," he said, not removing his mask. "They've been looking at Justin's junk balls for five innings. Throw hard strikes."

Duane nodded. The next pitch was fouled off. Then the batter swung and missed and with the count 2–2, Duane reared back and threw a blistering fastball chest high. The batter swung but he didn't have a chance. Strike three.

"Aiieeee!" came a war cry from Nick to lead the cheers.

"Smoke city!"

"Beauty, beauty, beauty!"

Now there were two outs.

Funny thing about baseball. One pitch can change a whole game. After getting ahead on the count 0–

1, Duane tried to put something extra on the old number one. It slipped out of his hand just a split second too early and made a beeline for the batter. The Lincoln man knew exactly what to do. He took one for the team, twisting, but not jumping away to avoid the pitch. It hit him and the umpire didn't hesitate. He pointed to first. Happily rubbing his shoulder, the batter jogged to first, while the runners advanced and Lincoln took an 8–7 lead.

Duane was devastated. He hung his head in disgust. Dennis walked half-way out to the mound, but couldn't think of what to say. Dennis himself was just as devastated. The comeback was shot. He tossed Duane the ball and returned to the plate.

Duane got the next batter to ground out to short for the third out. Alden had three outs left. Barry, Kyle, and Mitch were on deck.

Barry hit a line drive but the pitcher stuck out his glove and snagged it. A pure instinct play. One out.

Kyle drove a ball deep to left, but it hooked foul. It was deep enough for a home run, but it was nothing but an impressive strike. Two pitches later he topped a pitch for an easy grounder to third. Two out.

Mitch took a ball and a strike before hitting a long fly to right. Three out—and that's all you get. Alden had lost and the season was over. It could have been a great comeback. It could have been a lot of things. But it wasn't. And they don't hand out trophies inscribed "could have been."

"You proved a lot to me, and I hope to yourselves, by battling back the way you did," Coach Lanigan said to the gathered players in the locker room. "We had our ups and downs this year, but today you showed me real guts. It makes me feel good about next year."

As the players unpacked their lockers into their duffel bags for the last time, the room was quiet. After all the squabbles and pranks and name-calling, they had finally gotten it right. They *could* play ball together. But now it was over and despite everything, they were sad to be going.

18

Dennis had little time to reflect on the baseball season. He had final exams to prepare for, just a week away now. It was strange getting home at three-thirty in the afternoon after two months of practicing every day. But now Dennis had time to relax for a change.

When the final bell rang on the last day of school, Dennis was happy. His first year at Alden had been a good one. He had been afraid that all the new people might have meant that the gang—Nick, Justin, Sam, and he—would have split up, but they hadn't. Playing on real teams had been great. The basketball team had won the championship, and even though they hadn't done so well in football or baseball, both teams showed potential. School had been okay, too. His grades were all right, and there were plenty of girls he was friends with, even if he didn't specifically have a "girlfriend." Maybe next year.

The first day of summer vacation, Dennis just sat and zoned out watching TV until his head hurt. Then he watched some more. It felt great to do nothing. The next day, he went down to the Fairwood Elementary School field to meet Nick, Sam, Justin, Dave, and a few other guys. They were getting up a baseball game.

He thought he might have been sick of baseball after the constant practices, but this was different. This was just for fun.

When Dennis rolled his ten-speed up to the backstop only Sam had arrived. They starting tossing the ball and talking.

"Did you sign up for Algonquin League yet?" Sam asked. In Cranbrook the Algonquin League was next after you were too old for Little League.

"Not yet. You?"

"Yeah. You better do it soon."

"When does it start?"

"Next week some time."

"Are Nick and Justin signed up?"

"No, they're both going to camp."

"Camp?"

"Yeah," Sam said, "it's some kind of soccer camp. An overnight camp at State University. Justin was trying to talk me into going with him, but I'm just not that crazy about soccer."

Nick and Dave arrived, stacked their bikes against the fence and joined them.

"So, Justin got you to go to camp with him?" Sam asked.

"Yeah, he twisted my arm." Nick laughed. "It should be fun."

"Maybe I should come, too. Soccer's a blast," Dennis put in.

Justin arrived next.

"Hey, Justin!" Nick yelled. "Dennis just said he'd come to soccer camp with us."

"Right!" Justin said, putting on his glove. "You can't fool me. I know he and Sam are going to play Algonquin League, right?"

Dennis and Sam nodded.

"Well," Justin began. "I heard that thirteen-year-olds hardly get to play in the games, since you're on the same team with fourteen-year-olds," Justin said.

"Maybe most thirteen-year-olds, but we're so good they'll have to play us," Sam said.

"You should be practicing football all summer, Sam," Dennis said. "Otherwise we're not going to have a chance in the fall."

"Don't worry about me," Sam blustered.

"Let's play 500—I'll hit first," Dennis suggested, and the others headed into the outfield.

They had only been playing a couple of minutes when Dennis noticed Duane down the street on his bike. Dennis picked up a ball and hit a long fly. Then he looked at Duane again. It looked as if he had stopped and turned around, but after the next ball Dennis hit, he saw that Duane had turned back and was coming in their direction. As Duane came closer Dennis saw he had his glove with him. Dennis waved.

Duane acted like he had just noticed them, but he was a bad actor.

"Wanna play?" Dennis asked. "Always room for one more."

"Oh? Yeah, sure." Duane said, slowing down, then parking his bike.

Dennis kept hitting balls while Duane took a spot in the outfield. He was glad Duane had come along. Dennis didn't care how many friends he had—Nick, Justin, and Sam were enough—but he did care about having enemies: the fewer the better. Anyway, it was true about 500, there was always room for one more.

Dave caught a pop to win and came running in to take over the batting. Dennis took his place next to Duane in the outfield.

"Playing Algonquin, Duane?" he asked.

"Yeah, you?"

"I think so."

Dave hit a liner that Sam fielded on one hop.

"Good of you to let me play after I blew our last game," Duane said.

They all just laughed. Dave hit a pop and Nick got under it, but Sam jumped in and stole the catch.

"Hey, I was the one who loaded the bases," Justin said.

"That's right," Duane said, pretending to remember. "It was *your* fault. I feel better now."

They laughed again.

The six of them played the game until the sun was low in the sky and their shadows were long against the uncut outfield grass. Someone had started a cookout and they could smell the charcoal smoke. It reminded them that it was dinnertime, so they took a few last tosses and broke up the game. Then they each hooked their gloves onto their handlebars and pedaled home.